The
Donner Party

CORNERSTONES OF FREEDOM

SECOND SERIES

Roger Wachtel

Children's Press®
A Division of Scholastic Inc.
New York • Toronto • London • Auckland • Sydney
Mexico City • New Delhi • Hong Kong
Danbury, Connecticut

Photographs © 2003: Bancroft Library, University of California, Berkeley: 42 (BANC MSS/C-E 176), 30, 45 center left (Charles F. McGlashen Papers, BANC MSS C-B 570), 41 (Charles F. McGlashen Papers, BANC MSS C-B 570, folder 110); Beinecke Rare Book and Manuscript Library, Yale Collection of American Literature: 36, 45 bottom; California State Department of Parks and Recreation, Donner Memorial State Park: 38; California State Department of Parks and Recreation, Sutters Fort State Historic Park: 7, 15, 16, 25, 44 top; California State Library, Sacramento, California, California History Room: 32; California State Parks: 12, 31, 37 right, 37 left, 45 center right; Corbis Images: 29, 33 (Bettmann), 8 (MAPS.com), 20, 26, 28; Hulton|Archive/Getty Images: cover top, 10, 13, 34, 44 bottom right; Huntington Library, San Marino, California: 24 (Elizabeth Poor Donner Houghton Papers, #HM58189); Illinois State Historical Society: 6; Library of Congress: 5, 11, 17, 44 bottom left; National Archives and Records Administration: 19; North Wind Picture Archives: cover bottom, 9, 45 top; Scotts Bluff National Monument, Gering, NE: 13 ("Approaching Chimney Rock", by William Henry Jackson); Superstock, Inc./Christies Images: 3, 4; Utah State Historical Society: 22; Wyoming State Archives: 18.

Library of Congress Cataloging-in-Publication Data
Wachtel, Roger.
  The Donner Party / Roger Wachtel.
    p. cm. — (Cornerstones of freedom. Second series)
  Summary: Recounts the journey of the Donner Party which, in 1846, sought to travel from Independence, Missouri, to California but took an untried shortcut that trapped them in the Sierra Nevada mountains during a terrible winter.
  Includes bibliographical references and index.
    ISBN 0-516-24218-0
    1. Donner Party—Juvenile literature. 2. Pioneers—California—Biography—Juvenile literature. 3. Pioneers—West (U.S.)—Biography—Juvenile literature. 4. Overland journeys to the Pacific—Juvenile literature. 5. Frontier and pioneer life—West (U.S.)—Juvenile literature. [1. Donner Party. 2. Pioneers. 3. Overland journeys to the Pacific. 4. Survival.] I. Title. II. Series.
F868.N5W33 2003
979.4'03—dc21

                              2003005615

1 2 3 4 5 6 7 8 9 10 R 12 11 10 09 08 07 06 05 04 03

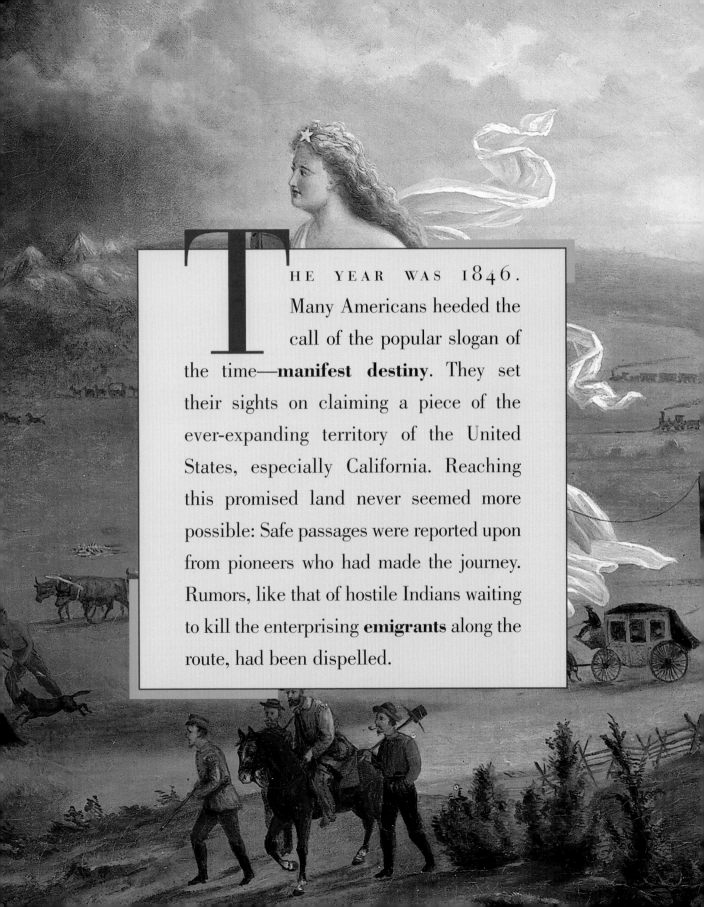

THE YEAR WAS 1846. Many Americans heeded the call of the popular slogan of the time—**manifest destiny**. They set their sights on claiming a piece of the ever-expanding territory of the United States, especially California. Reaching this promised land never seemed more possible: Safe passages were reported upon from pioneers who had made the journey. Rumors, like that of hostile Indians waiting to kill the enterprising **emigrants** along the route, had been dispelled.

The Donner party was one of the many westward-bound emigrant parties that year. However, the three families and their numerous traveling partners decided to take a shortcut described in a book by a man who had never actually taken the shortcut himself. It was a terrible mistake. What should have been a five-month journey took a year to complete, killed dozens, and stranded them in the mountains for the worst winter in history. This shortcut, they found, took longer than the accepted routes.

John Gast's painting *American Progress* symbolized the early-19th century belief that the United States needed to settle the lands west of the Mississippi River in order to fulfill its "manifest destiny."

* * * *

In the end, **emaciated** and delirious from months without real food, they resorted to the most terrible act any of them could imagine. They ate the dead, but they did so in shame, pained and horrified at what their mistake had forced them to do. And in doing so, they became one of the most famous groups to ever cross the American West.

THE PARTY GATHERS

The spring of 1846 was a busy time. Tensions between Mexico and the United States were escalating toward war over the United States' **annexation** of the Republic of Texas, which Mexico believed it owned. Americans were eager to bring other territories disputed with Mexico in the West under U.S. dominance. The Mormons began their journey to the Great Salt Lake this year, where they would settle and safely practice their religion.

An estimated 1,500 people were expected to leave Independence, Missouri—a jumping off point—into "the Great American Desert." There would certainly be a lot of danger for these pioneers, but there was some comfort in numbers and the knowledge that others had already done it. Others accepted even more risk than was necessary.

The front page of *The California Star*, a San Francisco newspaper, carried one of the first accounts of the Donner party on April 10, 1847. "A more shocking scene cannot be imagined," the newspaper's story began, and went on to describe bones and bodies of half-eaten flesh in the snow around the cabins at Donner Lake.

5

Springfield, Illinois, the hometown of the Donner and Reed families, looked like this in 1846. Among its leading citizens at the time was a tall, thin lawyer and acquaintance of James Reed by the name of Abraham Lincoln.

In Springfield, Illinois, three families were making the final preparations for their journey. The brothers George and Jake Donner and their families made a total of 16 all together. They were farmers looking for the free, fertile land they had heard was available in California. They planned to settle around the bay of San Francisco. The organizer was a 45-year-old businessman named James Frazier Reed. His first wife had died and he was now married to Margaret, 32, who had lost her first husband to cholera. She had a daughter, Virginia, who was 13, from that first marriage, and she and James had three more children, Patty, 8, Jimmy, 5, and Thomas, 3.

Margaret suffered from terrible headaches. Her husband thought that a better climate might be the cure for these. Margaret's mother, Sarah Keyes, lived with them. She refused to be separated from her only daughter. She would accompany them on the journey, despite being in her 70s and terribly sick.

James and Margaret Reed were among the survivors of the Donner party expedition. They settled in San Jose, California, where James grew rich as a businessman. Margaret described her new home of California as "the greatest place for horse and cattle you ever saw."

While James, George, and Jake had moved many times, they had never done anything like this. They were about to travel 2,500 miles, much of it on foot. All their possessions, packed in wagons, would be pulled by oxen. Oxen were preferred over horses by the westward-bound settler. They were less expensive, could live off a diet of sage and prairie grass found along the way, and would willingly dredge through mud, as well as climb mountains and hills. However, the average rate of speed that a wagon could be pulled by oxen was no more than 2 miles per hour.

Still, these men could not do this alone. Seven teamsters answered George's advertisement, which promised free

THE OREGON TRAIL

A 20-mile-wide gap in the treacherous Rocky Mountains known as South Pass made possible the settling of what are now the states of Nevada, California, Utah, Idaho, Oregon, and Washington. Though previously known, it was the report back east in 1825 by a mountain man that led to the true forging of the Oregon Trail. The first covered wagon took to the 2,000-mile trail in 1836. The first massive migration of roughly 1,000 pioneers took place in 1843.

This map shows the Donner party's route west, as well as the Oregon and California trails.

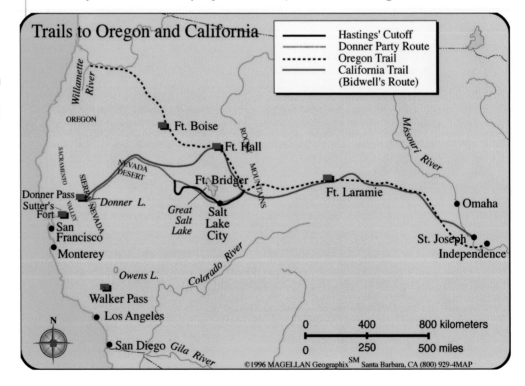

Because horses were too valuable to be used as draft animals, oxen were the animals used most often to pull the settlers' wagons. The illness, injury, or death of one of these animals, as in this 19th-century illustration, could mean serious trouble for an emigrant party.

passage to California in exchange for their help driving the wagons. The Reeds also took two hired servants, making the initial group 32 strong.

TO INDEPENDENCE AND BEYOND

With nine brand-new covered wagons, the Donner party left Springfield in April and headed to Independence, Missouri.

A pioneer woman wields a whip alongside an ox-drawn wagon train in this 19th-century photograph.

TEAMSTERS

Teamsters were men who were skilled at working a team of animals. They usually plodded along side them, leading the yokes. "Giddup! Gee! Haw! Whoa!" they would shout as they cracked the whip to keep them in line. Travelers heading west often hired teamsters to help with the journey. It was about the only way a poor, single man could get to the West, due to the expense of supplies needed for the journey.

Independence was one of the first small towns encountered along the Missouri River. Many pioneers would have loaded their wagons onto steamships in St. Louis for the 200-mile journey upstream. Independence was the most popular of several "jumping off" points into the West. Here, information both true and false about the journey ahead was shared. People rushed around making sure they had everything they needed. They organized groups of larger parties with which to travel. The town was as busy as a large city. Its economy depended on these emigrants.

* * * *

THE
EMIGRANTS' GUIDE,

TO

OREGON AND CALIFORNIA,

CONTAINING SCENES AND INCIDENTS OF A PARTY OF

OREGON EMIGRANTS;

A DESCRIPTION OF OREGON;

SCENES AND INCIDENTS OF A PARTY OF CALIFORNIA

EMIGRANTS;

AND

A DESCRIPTION OF CALIFORNIA;

WITH

A DESCRIPTION OF THE DIFFERENT ROUTES TO

THOSE COUNTRIES;

AND

ALL NECESSARY INFORMATION RELATIVE TO THE

EQUIPMENT, SUPPLIES, AND THE METHOD

OF TRAVELING.

———————

BY LANSFORD W. HASTINGS,

Leader of the Oregon and California Emigrants of 1842.

———————

PROVISIONS

Supplies for the journey cost between $700 and $1,500. The average family of four required over 1,000 pounds of food for the journey. The suggested provisions included 200 pounds of flour, 150 pounds of bacon, 10 pounds of coffee, 20 pounds of sugar, and 10 pounds of salt. All of this would be carried in the wagon. Sometimes, cows were brought to provide milk and butter. Weapons, such as guns and tools, were also necessary.

This is the title page of Lansford Hastings' *Emigrants' Guide to California and Oregon.* Eager to attract American settlers to California, Hastings recommended a shortcut to California that no one, before the Donner party, had ever tried to travel with a wagon train.

Described as "handsome, strong-faced, quick and intelligent of speech," Lansford Hastings was a lawyer from Ohio who dreamed of liberating California from Mexico and establishing it as an independent nation, where he would become its first president.

Deciding when to leave for the West was crucial. Travelers had to leave after the spring rains that made the roads impassable and after the grass had had time to grow, so that the oxen could graze. But there were mountains on the other end of the trip. If they reached them after the early winter snow, they could get caught there. Getting to the mountains late could be deadly.

The Oregon Trail led from Independence through the Midwest along the Platte River to the Rockies through Utah, Wyoming, and Idaho down the Columbia River into Willamette Valley in Oregon. Those going to California often went the same way, turning south into the Sacramento River Valley. Though it was treacherous and often deadly, it was the tested and accepted way to go.

James Reed and the Donners had read *The Emigrants' Guide to Oregon and California* by Lansford Hastings. Hastings was a lawyer from Ohio who had been to California in 1842. He was aware that California was most likely going to be taken from Mexico by the United States. If he could promote enough eastern Americans to this beautiful land, guiding them there himself, perhaps he would be seen as a sort of hero, and rewarded accordingly.

Hastings described a short cut that would take weeks off the trip on pages 137–138 of *The Emigrants' Guide*. "The most direct route, for the California emigrants, would be to leave the Oregon route, about 200 miles east from Fort Hall; thence bearing west southwest, to the Salt Lake; and thence continuing down to the bay of St. Francisco, by the route just described." It seemed like this shortcut would work,

* * * *

but no one, not even Hastings himself, had ever tried it. In fact, on the same day the Donners left Springfield, Hastings was himself leaving from California to see what his shortcut was really like. Unfortunately for the Donners, they found that out far too late.

HEADING WEST

The party left Independence on May 12, 1846, but they weren't alone. They joined another group of wagons that was going west. They would travel with them to the cutoff that Hastings described in his book, in what is now the southwest corner of Wyoming. Soon after they left, riders reached them with mail and word that war had broken out between the United States and Mexico.

A 19th-century depiction of the Battle of Monterrey in the Mexican War. At the time of the battle, the Donner party was struggling across the Great Salt Lake Desert.

WAGONS

Most emigrant families used small farm wagons, measuring about ten feet long and three-and-a-half feet wide, to cross the West. Every aspect of the wagon was carefully designed for crossing the unique geography and weather conditions they would encounter. Smaller wheels in front than in back helped with turning sharp corners. Wide wheels moved quicker in soft, sandy soil. Cotton covers could be closed at each end to keep out dust and were treated with linseed oil to keep out the rain.

A wagon train comes to a halt for the night. As one can see in the background, the wagons would often be arranged in a circle at night. The families would cook, eat, and sleep inside the circle while the wagons served as a barricade against attack.

The early going was slow and tedious. One problem may have been over-packing. Many emigrants heading west made this error. They made haste to throw things out alongside the trail they felt they could live without. In the case of the Donner Party, another problem could have been what thirteen-year-old Virginia Reed called her family's "pioneer palace car." It was a two-story wagon with built-in beds. It even had a stove. It was big and heavy and slow, and extra oxen had to be hooked to it to get it up many hills.

One of the reasons the wagon was so luxurious was to make Margaret's mother, Sarah Keyes, more

DAILY LIFE ALONG THE TRAIL

Every one over the age of five would have duties along the route. Women cooked, mended, did laundry, and tended to the children. Men tended to the animals, maintained the wagons, and hunted. Boys helped their fathers and girls would mostly help their mothers, especially with setting out utensils and then cleaning and repacking them. Everyone sat together on the ground and ate dinner in the evenings. Then, a bonfire was built. The children played ball and tag. Adults would share stories, and sing songs, which sometimes led to everyone dancing!

This small, wooden doll belonged to eight-year-old Patty Reed. Like its owner, it survived the winter in the Sierra Nevada and made it to California.

comfortable. She was very sick, however, and died early in the trip, on May 27.

The Reeds and the others mourned Sarah's death, but there was no time to spare. They buried her under a tree near present-day Alcove Springs, Kansas, and continued on. Virginia missed her grandmother, writing, "Every time we come into the wagon, we look at the bed for her." Tamsen Donner tempted fate, writing in her journal that same night that the journey was much easier than she thought it would be.

They made steady progress for another month, coming to the settlement at Fort Laramie on June 27th in present-day eastern Wyoming. They were one week behind schedule. By then they had been joined by a number of families. The Breens and Dolans joined them, and a widow, Laviniah Murphy, and her daughters and sons-in-law. The Eddys were a young couple with small children. William Eddy was a helpful addition, since he was a skilled hunter and carriage maker who helped repair wagons. The Graves were so poor that the adults walked without shoes on and disliked the Reeds for their wealth. It is not certain how Charles Stanton came to be in the party, but he would prove to be very important to the group later on.

Margaret and Patrick Breen and their oldest son, John, (from left) were among the most popular members of the Donner party. Margaret and Patrick Breen had been born in Ireland and had only recently become U.S. citizens.

WARNINGS AND PROMISES

He didn't know it at the time, but just after June 27, James Clyman almost saved the Donner Party all of the pain they would suffer over the next several months. Clyman, a **mountain man**, had known James Reed in Illinois. He had just come from California using Hastings' short cut. They met and camped together. Reed was concerned about the time they had lost, and was eager for news of the cut off.

"I told them about the great desert and the roughness of the Sierras," Clyman would later remember, "and that a straight route might turn out to be impracticable. I told him to take the regular wagon track by way of Fort Hall (near present-day Pocatello, Idaho) and never leave it. It is barely possible to get through if you follow it and may be impossible if you don't." But Reed was concerned about the time already lost and convinced by Hastings' writing. He also thought that, bad as it might be, it would still be shorter. He ignored Clyman's warning. A few days later, the Donner party, nine families plus 16 men traveling alone, left Fort Laramie toward Sutter's

Originally from Wisconsin, James Clyman had already spent many years in the West as a mountain man by the time he encountered the Donner party at Fort Laramie in late June 1846. An acquaintance of James Reed, he warned the party not to take the Hastings cutoff.

The scrubby left fork in this early 20th-century photograph led the Donner party away from the main route toward Fort Hall and toward Fort Bridger and the Hastings cutoff.

LEADERSHIP ON THE TRAIL

Wagon parties were often all alone on the prairie, so they elected a captain who called meetings and led the decision-making process. People often traveled together who were virtual strangers, and after a time, there would often be disputes between members. The captain helped settle these.

Fort in the Sacramento Valley of California. They were still accompanied by others traveling west, but that, too, would soon change.

Then came a promise that raised their spirits. On July 17, a rider appeared with a letter from Lansford Hastings himself. It said that anyone on the road should stay together and head toward Fort Bridger, a trading post owned by frontiersman Jim Bridger, in what is now southwestern Wyoming. Fort Bridger was the last place to stock up on supplies before reaching California. There, Hastings would meet them and

18

take them through the shortcut. A day later, they crossed the Continental Divide. They were committed now. No turning back, but still 1,000 miles from their destination.

On July 20, they came to the Little Sandy River. Anyone taking the usual route would turn north. Those trying Hastings' cutoff would have to go south. Almost the entire train headed north. Just 20 wagons, including the Donners' and the Reeds' headed south. As they did, the newly smaller group met to elect a captain. Though James Reed had been their leader for the entire trip, many had grown tired of him. Others were jealous of his wealth. They elected George Donner instead.

They arrived at Fort Bridger to a broken promise. Lansford Hastings had already left, taking a wagon train with him. He left word that those arriving later should follow.

This 1867 photograph indicates what the Donner party would have encountered in trying to get their wagons across the Nevada desert.

As a dog (lower left) noses about the carcass of a dead ox, emigrants help their own draft animals by pushing the wagon on an uphill stretch of the trail.

The party decided to rest for four days. On July 31, James Reed wrote, "Hastings' cutoff is said to be saving 350 or 400 miles and a better route. The rest of the Californians went the long route, afraid of Hastings' cutoff. But Mr. Bridger informs me that it is a fine, level road with plenty of water and grass. It is estimated that 700 miles will take us to Captain Sutter's fort, which we hope to make seven weeks from this day." They moved through the cutoff that day, but it would be nine months before the last of the survivors would reach their destination.

THE CUTOFF

At first, they made steady progress, 10-12 miles a day. But they soon approached steep hills that the wagons could barely cross. Sometimes all of the oxen in the party would have to be used for each wagon. The sound of the wheels screeching across the rocky terrain sent a piercing echo for miles. By now they had reached Weber Canyon. On August 6, they found a note in the brush. It was from Hastings. It said the road ahead was impassable and that they should wait until he returned to show them a better way. James Reed set out alone to find him. He did, five days later, but Hastings refused to come back and help. He took Reed to the top of a mountain and showed him a trail he thought they should follow. Reed returned to the group and began to try and lead them through the tangle of Hastings' "better route."

The going then was terrible. Deep in the Wasatch Mountains, they struggled to make two miles a day. The men had to go ahead to chop the brush by hand, then come back for the others, over and over again. In one six-day period, they traveled only eight miles. They thought they would have to abandon the wagons, but incredibly hard work kept the train together.

What should have taken a week, took a month. Their mood was terrible, and now they had to go into the Great Salt Lake Desert. Many blamed Reed, but there were still 600 miles to go and they were now dangerously behind. Then someone found a note. It was in pieces, but it was from Hastings. "Two days . . . two nights . . . hard driving . . . across desert . . . reach water" was all they could make out. They took on as much water and grass as they could and headed out into the salt flats.

THE SALT DESERT

The Great Salt Lake in Utah is a remnant of Lake Bonneville, a prehistoric lake that was ten times larger than the 1,700-square-mile area of the modern-day Great Salt Lake. Four rivers flow into the lake, carrying minerals. However, the Great Salt Lake is a terminal lake, which means it has no outlet. When the water evaporates, a desert of salt is left behind where few animals and almost no plants can grow.

Although this photograph of the Great Salt Lake Desert was not taken until the 1920s, it still shows rusted wheel hubs from abandoned wagons, possibly those of the Donners.

INTO THE DESERT

Even today, a man in great condition, rested, and well-fed could die if he was caught in the salt desert of Utah. Indeed, the Donner party was about to embark across one of the most dangerous places on Earth.

They had been told that they could get through the desert in two days, but that was impossible. In temperatures that can exceed 100° Farenheit, the moisture under the surface of the ground would boil to the surface, creating a soup. The wagon wheels sank to their hubs. The animals worked so hard that they used up their water in two days. On the third night, the Reed's oxen ran off, crazed with thirst. The Reeds took what they could carry and set off on foot, abandoning the "pioneer palace car." At night, they had to sleep on the ground with their dogs on top of them to keep from freezing from the cold winds. In the desert, there are no trees or grass to hold the heat in. During the daytime, they nearly died from the intense heat.

It took five days to cross the desert. They did the final three days and nights with no water at all. They had been told it was 40 miles, but it was 80. Many almost died of thirst, and they lost 36 oxen. At a spring near the base of Pilot Mountain, they quenched their thirst for the first time in days. Some families were now on foot, their wagons far behind.

Their situation was terrible. Some simply fell to the ground praying and crying. Others cursed Hastings for his broken promises and lies. The Donner party was caught. It seemed there was no way to continue, but clearly they couldn't turn around and go the way they had come.

They were terrified, but they began to make their way now around the Ruby Mountain range in Nevada.

On September 26, they had made it back to where the shortcut met up with the main route to California, along the Humboldt River. As it turned out, not only was Hastings' cutoff more dangerous and difficult, it was also 125 miles longer than the accepted route. The travelers who had been led by Hastings himself were safely at Sutter's Fort by then. Only the Donners remained on the trail.

THE PARTY COMES APART

There weren't enough provisions to make it to California, so Charles Stanton volunteered to ride ahead to California and bring back help. The rest of the party continued toward the mountains. On October 5, as the party climbed a narrow, uphill path, John Snyder and James Reed argued when Snyder began beating oxen that had become entangled. Nerves on edge, the two men fought. Snyder hit Reed in the head, wounding him. When Snyder raised his hand a second time, Reed drew a knife and killed him.

Most of the party hated Reed. Many thought him arrogant. Others blamed him for following Hastings' route. They declared his act murder. One man, Lewis Keseberg, made a device to hang him. Margaret begged for mercy, and the group decided to banish him. He refused at first, but there was no choice. The next day he buried Snyder, said goodbye to his family, and rode out of camp.

Though small and wiry, Charles Stanton, a 35-year-old bachelor from Chicago by way of Brooklyn and Syracuse, New York, distinguished himself by his selfless attempts to get help for the trapped party.

WAGON TRAIN JUSTICE

There were no policemen or judges on the trails. When a rule or law was broken, the captain helped the members of the party decide on a punishment. Serious crimes could be punished with banishment (the offender would be forced to travel alone), or even execution.

According to some accounts, it was William Eddy who proposed that James Reed be isolated from the rest of the party after the gruesome fight that resulted in the death of John Snyder at Reed's hands. Because he was a wagonmaker and an excellent hunter, Eddy was a particularly valuable member of the Donner party.

The train went on. Most walked now as their oxen could barely pull the wagons. On October 7, Keseberg threw his friend, a man named Hardkoop, out of his wagon. Hardkoop was nearly 70, and fell behind quickly. Some boys were sent to find him, but by then he was five miles back. His feet were so swollen that the skin had split open. Several of the party went to Keseberg and begged him to help Hardkoop, but he refused. No longer a party, the group had begun to take care of only themselves. Hardkoop was left to die on the trail.

The Donner party encountered the Paiute Indians in what is now the state of Utah. The Paiutes were traditionally hunters and gatherers who survived on nuts, roots, berries, and small animals. Whites sometimes referred to the Paiutes as the "Diggers."

Then, one of Laviniah Murphy's sons-in-law was accidentally shot to death, and another man named Wolfinger died under mysterious circumstances. Unable to carry his possessions anymore, he decided to bury them by the trail. He hoped to come back and get them in better weather the next year. The men who stayed to help him returned without him, saying Indians had killed him. One of them, however, Joseph Reinhardt, eventually admitted to killing him, and others in the train, including Keseberg, were seen with his possessions.

* * * *

If dealing with tensions with each other was not enough, there was a surging threat with the local Native Americans. They were now in Digger Indian country. The Digger Indians were made up of fragments of Shoshone, Paiute, and other Great Basin tribes. They were hostile toward the white settlers because of their previous encounters with mountain men, who killed their members for sport. Diggers began raiding the Donner Party camps along the Humboldt, shooting their oxen with poison arrows, eventually killing twenty-one of them.

Clearly all that they had been through had taken its toll. There was constant bickering and disputes were common. They were starving and running out of time and they all knew it. Soon the way to Sutter's Fort would be full of snow and impassable.

A FINAL HOPE AND LINGERING DESPAIR

On October 19, though, there was great news. Charles Stanton returned with two of the best Indian guides from Sutter's Fort and mules loaded with food. He also brought word that the pass through the Sierra Nevada would be clear for another month. It seemed they were going to make it to California after all.

They rested for five days for the final march, but when they got under way again, more disaster struck. The axle on George Donner's wagon broke, and while he was fixing it, he suffered a gash on his hand. They fell behind as he dealt with the injury, which would soon become infected.

The western portion of the
Sierra Nevada is especially
rugged. Terrain that might
be passable by a man on
horseback or on foot was
much more difficult, if not
impossible, to cross for
heavily laden wagon trains.

The Breens and Kesebergs pushed ahead, followed by Stanton and the Reeds. On October 31, as they camped near the summit, a storm came in. The next morning the party tried to make it through the pass, but five feet of snow had already accumulated. The wagons wouldn't make it. Stanton and the Indians made it to the summit, but gave up. There was no one to lead them through. The party huddled against wind and snow.

By the next morning, the pass was completely closed. The Donner party was caught, only one day from safely passing through the mountains, 150 miles from their destination. The first two groups backtracked to a nearby lake and tried to set up a winter camp. Farther down the mountain, the two Donner families did the same. Neither had much food, and none were prepared for the ordeal they were about to experience.

INFECTION

There were rarely doctors and medication on the trail. People did not wash very often, so even small injuries, especially cuts and scrapes, could quickly become infected. In some cases, a cut that would heal in a week today would result in death.

In this illustration from an early account of the expedition, members of the Donner party construct cabins for winter shelter near present-day Donner Lake high in the Sierra Nevada. This drawing was based on a description given by William Murphy, a member of the Donner party.

Donner Lake was known as Truckee Lake before the Donner party spent its tragic winter there. Although this photograph was taken several decades after that fateful season, it shows the ruggedness of the terrain in which the pioneers found themselves.

THE FORLORN HOPE

The majority of the party took over some abandoned cabins near Truckee Lake. Others built simple shelters against the sides of what buildings were there. Six miles away, on Alder Creek, the Donners camped out in tents and waited for help that didn't come. There were attempts to get through the pass again, but the snow drifts had grown to 20 feet.

They ate what was left of the animals, even their pet dogs. The party took to mixing meat with hides, sticks, and earth, anything to stretch the little food they had and hold off starvation. On the night of December 15, Bayliss Williams, a teamster of the Reeds, starved to death. At the Donner camp, Jacob Donner, along with three other single men, had also perished.

It was time for drastic action. A party of the strongest travelers decided to go through the pass and get help. Nine men, including the two Indians, five women, and a twelve-year-old boy, were chosen. They called themselves "the Forlorn Hope." They took starvation rations, but after six days they were out of food. They also suffered from snow blindness, a temporary condition caused from the sun's ultraviolet rays reflected in the snow. Charles Stanton, too weak to continue, sat down in the snow and smoked his pipe as the rest went on without him.

Nine days out, the most horrible plan was made. The Forlorn Hope was lost and its members were dying. Someone made a suggestion perhaps they all were instinctively thinking. If one were to die, they could eat the meat of his body and the rest could survive.

That night the storm increased and the fire went out. William Eddy gathered everyone together and pulled blankets over them. By the morning, Patrick Dolan, Billy Graves, Lem Murphy, the youngest of the party, and Antonio, a teamster hired in Independence, had died. Someone cut meat off

This picture of Harriet Murphy Pike was taken in California, years after the Donner party's misadventures. She was one of only seven members of the Forlorn Hope to survive.

CANNIBALISM

Cannibalism is when humans eat other humans' flesh. It is rare today, but for thousands of years it was practiced as a part of some cultures. Many cannibals believed eating parts of people preserved their spirits. There have been some more recent famous examples where people who were lost and starving ate the dead to survive.

31

the arms and legs of the dead. They built a fire, cooked the meat and ate it. As they did, they wept and refused to look at one another, ashamed of what they were doing. The Indians refused the meat, but those who did eat felt a little better. Even so, others died in the following days. As they did, the others took meat from their bodies, labeling it so no one would have to eat their relatives.

They continued on, still lost. When they ran out of meat, someone suggested killing the Indians and eating them. Hearing this, the two men quietly escaped into the woods. Later, the group found them dying in the snow. William Foster, insane with hunger, shot them, and their bodies were eaten.

On January 17, William Eddy stumbled out of the Sierra Nevada and into a small Native-American settlement with six other members of the Forlorn Hope right behind him. They were forty miles north of Sutter's Fort. Of the Forlorn Hope, all five women, but only two men, had survived.

In early January, the Mexican-American war had ended with a U.S. victory. This meant there would be young, strong men available for James Reed, who had made it through the pass ahead of the weather, to form a rescue party.

Although he behaved heroically in trying to get help for the stranded members of the party, hunger and desperation drove William Foster to kill for food two Native Americans who tried to help the rescuers.

* * * *

THE FIRST RESCUE

Meanwhile, at the lake, the Donner party was slowly dying. There was no meat left. Even the hides that had been used for roofing were finally used for food. Then on February 19, 1847, the first relief party arrived at the lake. One of the rescuers, Daniel Rhoades, remembered, "...no living thing except ourselves was in sight. We raised a loud hello. And then we saw a woman emerge from a hole in the snow ...several others made their appearance...They were gaunt with famine and I can never forget the horrible

Based on descriptions by William Murphy and other survivors, this illustration shows the first rescuers reaching the encampment at Donner Lake. "Are you men from California, or do you come from heaven?" one of the survivors asked the rescuers, who had crossed frozen Donner Lake (just beyond the opening in the trees) on snowshoes.

This is a rare 19th-century photograph of a wagon train making its way through the Sierra Nevada. The Sierra Nevada forms a rugged, towering barrier between the arid Great Basin region to the east and the more fertile valleys of California to its west.

ghastly sight they presented. The first woman spoke . . . 'Are you men from California, or do you come from heaven?'"

The ordeal of the Donner party, however, wasn't nearly over. The rescuers could only take 24 back with them. They only had enough provisions for the return trip to feed that many people. They would have to leave 31 behind with almost no food. The Breens volunteered to stay behind as did the Donners. George was too sick from his wound to move and Tamsen refused to leave his side.

Thomas Reed was too small to make the trip, and everyone, including his own mother, was too weak to carry him. His nine-year-old sister, Patty, volunteered to stay with him. It could be fatal for everyone in this first group to be held up by anyone who couldn't keep up. Margaret Reed was faced with a terrible choice: should she stay too or rejoin her husband? Aquila Glover, a rescuer, assured her he would go back for them. "Well, Ma, if you never see me again, do the best you can," Patty told her weeping mother.

The dying continued in the camp. Bodies lay in the snow covered with quilts. The survivors were each beginning to give in to the idea that survival might mean eating the dead. The first relief party was finding tough going as well. Two of the children had already died when they met James Reed coming the other way with the second relief party. He was overjoyed to see his wife and children, but continued on for the others. By the time he reached the lake, ten more had died and the cannibalism at Donner Lake had begun.

James Reed was stunned by what he found when he arrived. Bodies were everywhere, and many had been cut

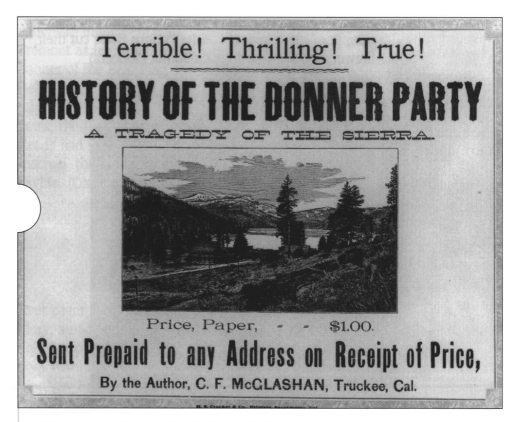

This is an advertisement for the first book about the Donner Party, written by Charles Fayette McGlashan and published in 1880. McGlashan was the editor of the *Truckee Republican*, a newspaper in Truckee, California, a small town that grew at the western end of what became known as the Donner Pass. McGlashan interviewed all the surviving members of the Donner Party for his book.

up for food. James later said, "[The survivors] looked more like demons than human beings."

The third relief party, led by a recovered Eddy and Foster, found only seven survivors. Unfortunately, their wives and sons were not among them. George and Tamsen were alive, but George was dying and Tamsen again refused to leave him. Her three daughters and Simon Murphy left with Eddy and Foster. Lewis Keseberg was too weak to travel.

The fourth and final party found only Keseberg. The others were all dead, and their bodies had kept him alive. When he reached safety at Johnson's Ranch in Bear Valley, California, it was April 25. It had been a year since the Donners and Reeds had left Springfield.

The adult Donners, whose name will forever be associated with cannibalism, all died. So did four of their children. All of the Reeds survived. Virginia wrote later of her pride that her family never ate human flesh.

In all, 41 of the 87 members of the Donner party died, as did the two Indians who had risked their lives to save them. Out of 55 males, 32 in the party died. Only 11 out of the 35 females perished. There may be a social explanation as to why more women and girls survived: unlike some of the males, none of the females traveled alone.

Like his married sister Harriet Murphy Pike, Billy Murphy (left) was one of the survivors of the Donner expedition. Eleanor Eddy, (right) William's wife, was 25 years old when the Donner party left Independence, Missouri.

They were all in family units and could draw upon each other for support. They fought to stay alive for the younger children. The males in the group were exposed to more risks as they exerted more energy on rescue missions, ensuring survival for all.

Most of the survivors became productive citizens of California. The orphaned children were adopted by local couples, and others settled in as they had planned to at the beginning of the trip. Margaret Reed's headaches, the family's main reason for leaving Illinois, stopped, as they

Eliza Donner (standing, at left) and Frances Donner (standing, at right) posed for this photo at the dedication of Donner State Memorial Park at Donner Lake. "There are enough errors to go around and there's enough heroism to go around," says an ancestor of one of the survivors about the ordeal of the Donner party.

had hoped they would. The next year gold was discovered near Sutter's Fort. Thousands of emigrants moved to California to get rich, but Hastings' cutoff was rarely used. Lansford Hastings died trying to start a colony of ex-Confederate soldiers in South America years later.

At first, the story of the Donner party traveled by word-of-mouth, newspapers, and letters. The *California Star* reported on the stranded travelers as early as February 1847.

On May 16, 1847, Virginia Reed, then fourteen, wrote a letter to her cousin, Mary Keyes, who lived back in Springfield, Illinois. No postal service was available in the West. Edwin Bryant, returning to Illinois for a visit, delivered the letter. Virginia described the yearlong ordeal to her cousin. She emphasized how none of her family ever ate the dead, and offered the now famous advice, "Remember, don't take no cutoffs and hurry along as fast as you can."

Most of what is known today comes from this account, the journals that some of the party members kept, and the survivors, after years of pain and silence, beginning to tell the story and reach out to find other survivors.

It is impossible to discuss the Donner party without discussing how they survived with no food. When the papers first told the story, they focused on the cannibalism, even suggesting that the survivors had grown to love the taste of human flesh. Nothing could be further from the truth. The survivors never bragged or boasted about what they resorted to for survival. It was in horror and desperation that they even did it, almost insane from hunger.

Their story is more about the choices they made—choices that seem to some now incredibly foolish. If they had taken the safe route, if they had listened to Clyman's warning, if they had rested just one day less at any point in the trip, few would even know the name Donner. Their story is about courage and honor. It is also about cowardice and dishonor. They were ordinary people under extraordinary stress.

John Breen, a teenager at the time, was given the task of burying the dead that ghastly winter. He was rescued with the third relief party. Thirty years later, he wrote in his memoirs:

> *It was long after dark when we got to Johnson's ranch, so the first time I saw it was early in the morning. The weather was fine. The ground was covered with green grass. The birds were singing from the tops of the trees and the journey was over. I could scarcely believe I was alive. The scene that I saw that morning seems to be photographed on my mind. Most of the incidents are gone from memory, but I can always remember the camp near Johnson's ranch.*

Martha Reed, known as Patty, was eight years old when she set out with her parents, James and Margaret Reed, for California in 1846. Seventy-two years later, she posed for this photograph at Donner Lake.

Patrick Breen's handwritten diary is one of the Donner party artifacts that survived the expedition. It is one of the primary sources of information about what happened in the course of that disastrous trip.

Diary
of
Patrick Breen
one of the
Donner Party
1846-7.
Presented by Dr Geo McKinstry
to
Bancroft Library

Glossary

annexation—when a government claims territory
     as its own

emaciated—thin or wasting away because of hunger or
     lack of food

emigrants—people who move from one place to another
     in search of work or opportunity, particularly
     within the same country

manifest destiny—the belief that it was the destiny of
     the United States to expand from the Atlantic
     Coast all the way to the Pacific Ocean

mountain man—one who made his living trapping
     fur-bearing animals and trading or selling their
     skins in the unexplored areas of the American
     West during the first half of the 19th century

Timeline: The Donner

1842 1846

Landsford Hastings travels to California. Eventually publishes *The Emigrants' Guide to Oregon and California* that would serves as the Donners' guide.

APRIL 16
The Donners and Reeds leave Springfield for Independence, Missouri.

MAY 12
What would become the Donner party leaves Independence traveling west toward California.

JUNE
Settlers in California rebel against Mexican government. Mexican War under way.

MAY 27
Sarah Keyes, Margaret Reed's mother, dies on the banks of the Big Blue River.

JUNE 27
Party reaches Fort Laramie. James Clyman tells James Reed to avoid the Hastings cutoff.

JULY 18
The party crosses the Continental Divide.

JULY 20
The Donner Party turns south toward Hastings' cutoff.

JULY 31
The party receives assurances that the cutoff is safe and easy.

AUGUST 22–30
The party leaves the mountains and heads into the desert. What should have taken a week had taken almost four.

AUGUST 5
After five days of crossing, the last three with no water, the party leaves the salt desert. Many wagons and more than 30 oxen are gone.

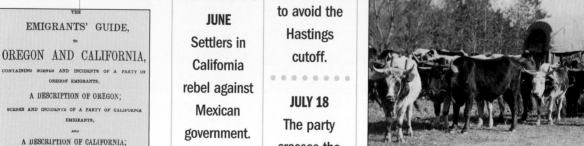

Party

1847

SEPTEMBER 26
Donner Party reaches the Humboldt River. This is where the long route and the shortcut meet.

OCTOBER 5
James Reed kills John Snyder. He is banished and continues to California.

OCTOBER 19
Charles Stanton returns from California with relief provisions. He assures the party they have a month before the pass into California and safety will be closed. James Reed reaches Sutter's Fort. All men are fighting the Mexicans, so no relief trip is made.

NOVEMBER 1
A snowstorm hits, trapping the Donner party for the winter.

MID-DECEMBER
The Forlorn Hope leaves to get help. Fifteen leave, of whom only seven will survive. They have cannibalized the dead for survival.

JANUARY 10
American troops win key battles near Los Angeles. Americans take California. James Reed organizes a rescue party.

JANUARY 17
Survivors of the Forlorn Hope are found.

FEBRUARY 19
The first relief team reaches the Donner Party. Twenty-four of the party are rescued.

LATE FEBRUARY
Second relief, by James Reed, arrives in camp. Survivors have begun eating the dead.

APRIL 25
The last survivors of the Donner party reach safety.

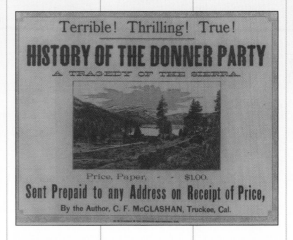

Terrible! Thrilling! True!
HISTORY OF THE DONNER PARTY
A TRAGEDY OF THE SIERRA.

Price, Paper, - - $1.00.

Sent Prepaid to any Address on Receipt of Price,

By the Author, C. F. McGLASHAN, Truckee, Cal.

To Find Out More

BOOKS AND VIDEOS

Burns, Ric. *The American Experience: The Donner Party.* PBS Video. 1992.

Burns, Ric. *The American Experience: The Way West.* PBS Video, 1992.

Calabro, Marian. *The Perilous Journey of the Donner Party.* Houghton Mifflin: New York, 1999.

On the Trail of Tragedy: The Excavation of the Donner Party Site. USDA Forest Service Videos, 1992.

ONLINE SITES

The American Experience: The Donner Party. Website of the PBS Series film on the Donner Party, includes maps and interview with the filmmakers.
http://www.pbs.org/wgbh/amex/donner/

The Donner Party by Daniel M. Rosen. Includes logs of members of the Donner Party.
http://www.members.aol.com/DanMRosen/donner/

Donner State Park. Website of the California State Park
http://www.ceres.ca.gov/sierradsp/donner.html

The Truckee-Donner Historical Society. Website of the historical society that preserves the history of the area.
http://www.truckeehistory.tripod.com

Index

About the Author

Roger Wachtel has been an educator for 17 years, first as a high school English teacher, then as a university instructor. He is now the writing specialist for the Peru Community Schools in Peru, Indiana. He was born in New Jersey, went to high school in Belgium, and now lives in Westfield, Indiana. He is married to Jeanette and has three sons, Thomas, Ben, and Josh. He has a Master's degree in English Education from Butler University. In his spare time, he reads and writes, follows the New York Mets passionately, and goes to automobile races with his sons and brothers.